OUR CHILDREN CAN SOAR

A Celebration of Rosa, Barack, and the Pioneers of Change

Michelle Cook • FOREWORD BY Marian Wright Edelman

ILLUSTRATIONS BY

Cozbi A. Cabrera • R. Gregory Christie • Bryan Collier
Pat Cummings • Leo and Diane Dillon • AG Ford
E. B. Lewis • Frank Morrison • James Ransome
Charlotte Riley-Webb • Shadra Strickland • Eric Velasquez

BLOOMSBURY

NEW YORK BERLIN LONDON

Published by Bloomsbury U.S.A. Children's Books
175 Fifth Avenue, New York, New York 10010

Library of Congress Cataloging-in-Publication Data
Cook, Michelle.
Our children can soar : a celebration of Rosa, Barack, and the pioneers of change /
by Michelle Cook ; illustrations by Cozbi Cabrera . . . [et al.]. — 1st ed.
p.   cm.
ISBN-13: 978-1-59990-418-4 • ISBN-10: 1-59990-418-7 (hardcover)
ISBN-13: 978-1-59990-419-1 • ISBN-10: 1-59990-419-5 (reinforced)
1. African Americans—Biography. 2. African American celebrities—Biography.
3. African Americans—History—20th century. I. Cabrera, Cozbi A., ill. II. Title.
E185.96.C67 2009   920'.009296073—dc22   2009001730

The artwork in this book was rendered in a variety of styles using
multiple mediums, including acrylics, watercolors, pastels, and collage.

First U.S. Edition 2009
Book design by Donna Mark
Printed in the U.S.A. by Worzalla
2 4 6 8 10 9 7 5 3 1 (hardcover)
2 4 6 8 10 9 7 5 3 1 (reinforced)

All papers used by Bloomsbury U.S.A. are natural, recyclable products
made from wood grown in well-managed forests. The manufacturing processes
conform to the environmental regulations of the country of origin.

FOREWORD

"Rosa sat so Martin could march. Martin marched so Barack could run. Barack ran so our children can soar!" When versions of this saying began circulating during the historic 2008 presidential election, they captured the belief that, just like Mrs. Rosa Parks and Dr. Martin Luther King Jr., President Barack Obama was part of a legacy of trailblazers and leaders—each of whom took a giant new step, building on the sweat, toil, struggle, and sacrifice of our slave forebears, to make a better nation for the next generation of black Americans and all Americans. Now this beautiful book has captured that message for our children. Dr. Carter G. Woodson, the scholar and historian called "the Father of Black History," taught us that "those who have no record of what their forebears have accomplished lose the inspiration which comes from the teaching of biography and history." From George Washington Carver to Ella Fitzgerald to Thurgood Marshall, each of the pioneers lovingly depicted here wrote a new chapter in African American and American history. *Our Children Can Soar* will help make sure all young people know their inspiring stories.

As families read this book together, I hope parents and grandparents will share their own memories about the people in their family trees who stood strong and laid the foundations for the generations that followed them. All of these stories bring history alive and reinforce the idea that anyone and *everyone* can use their lives to make a difference. Not everyone's name is written in the history books, but as *Our Children Can Soar* reminds us, African American history is the collective story of many, many people who never gave up and never turned around, but instead always quietly took that next step forward in faith so their children would be able to go even farther and have better lives. And they never lost their passion to help our nation honor its creed of freedom and justice for all. It is the story of hope. We need to teach today's children all of these rich lessons—and then stand behind and watch them soar.

—MARIAN WRIGHT EDELMAN

Our ancestors fought . . .

so George could invent.

George invented . . .

so Jesse could sprint.

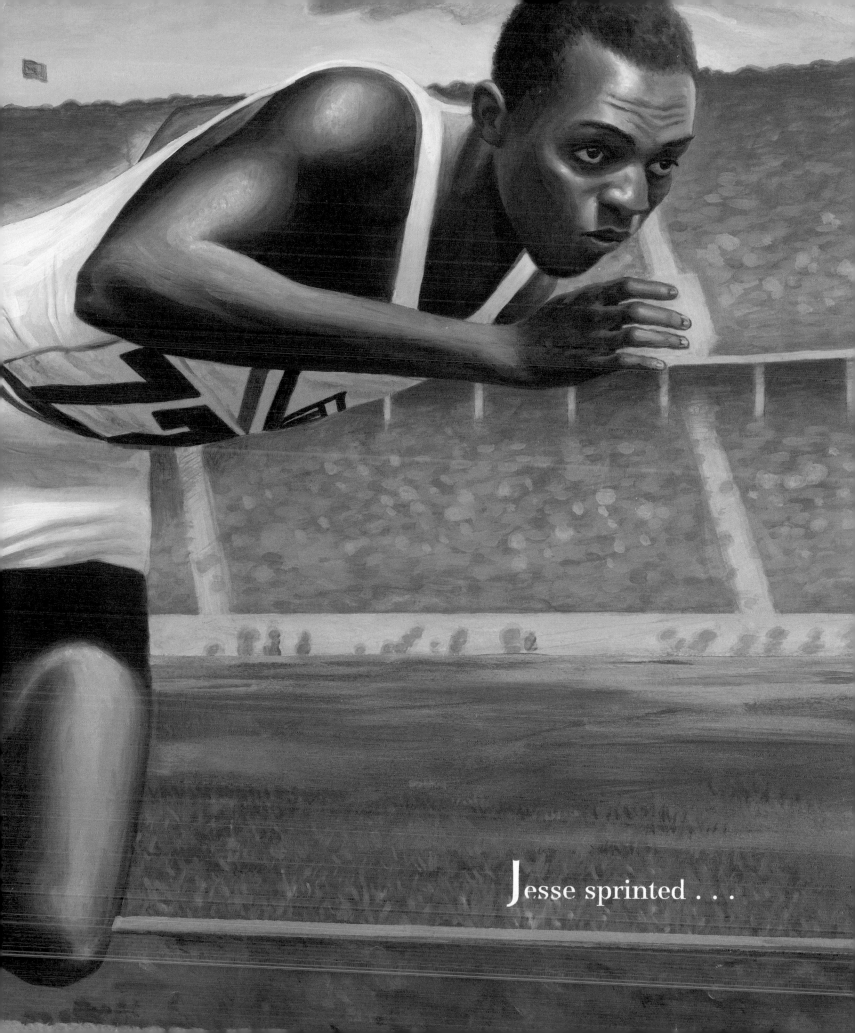

Jesse sprinted . . .

so Hattie could star.

Hattie starred . . .

so Ella could sing.

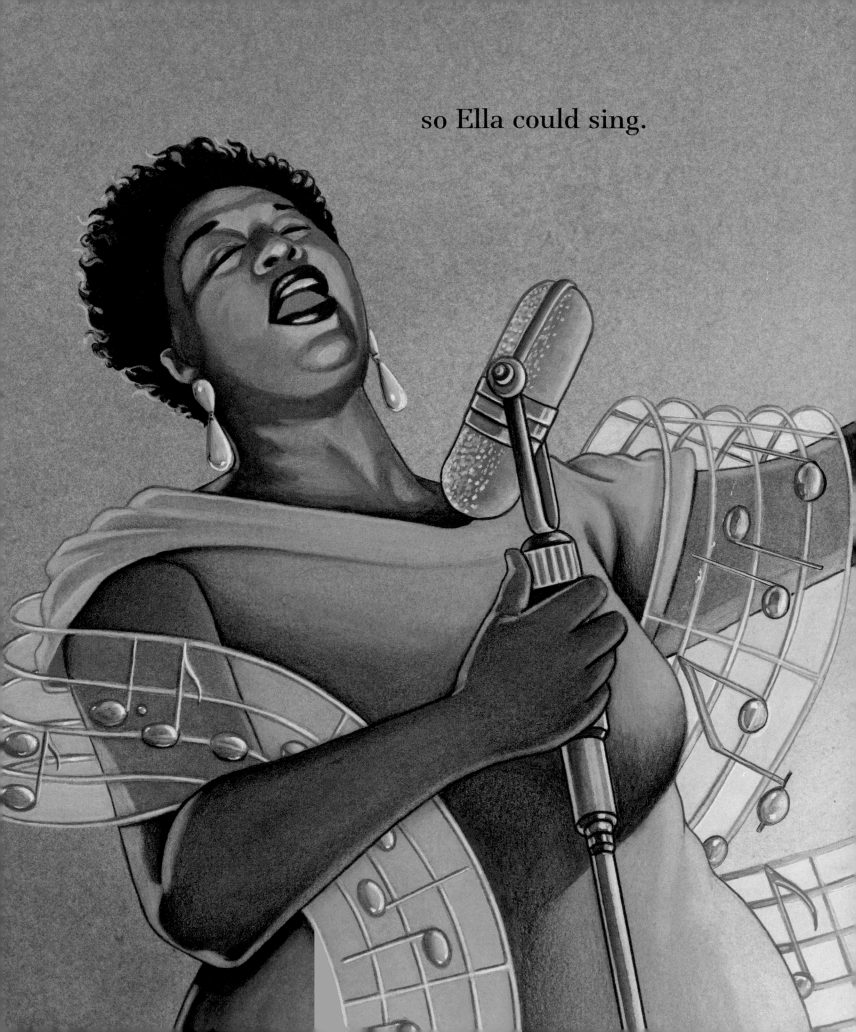

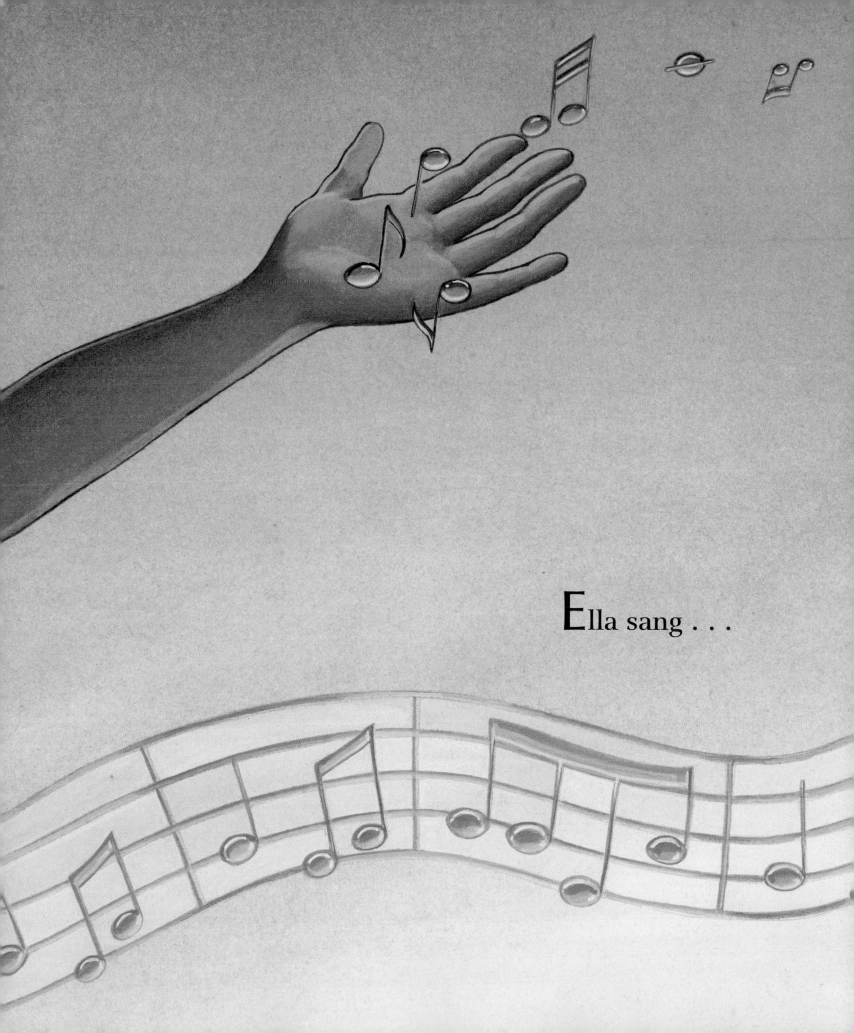

Ella sang . . .

so Jackie could score.

Jackie scored . . .

so Rosa could sit.

Rosa sat . . .

so Ruby could learn.

Ruby learned . . .

so Martin could march.

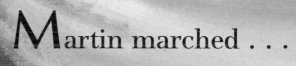

Martin marched . . .

so Thurgood could rule.

so our children can soar!

Barack ran . . .

so Barack could run.

And higher and faster and stronger they go.

THE PIONEERS OF CHANGE

GEORGE WASHINGTON CARVER (circa 1864–1943)

An accomplished botanist and chemist, George Washington Carver discovered hundreds of uses for the peanut, sweet potato, and soybean, among other plants. Though he was born into slavery, as a free man he went on to graduate college and earn a master's degree, ultimately becoming the director of agricultural research at Tuskegee University under Booker T. Washington. Carver was greatly concerned with the plight of Southern farmers, and he worked to reinvigorate soil depleted by cotton crops. His scientific research was second only to the contribution he made to society and education, working toward the betterment of African Americans in the post–Civil War era.

JESSE OWENS (1913–1980)

One of the most famous Olympians ever, Jesse Owens won four gold medals in track and field at the 1936 Berlin Olympics. Owens began breaking records in junior high school and high school and went on to compete at Ohio State University, where he most notably set three world records and tied a fourth all in one day. Though he was an athletic superstar, Owens had no scholarship and was forced to work menial jobs to pay his way through college and support his family. Owens's triumph at the Olympics was legendary: his four gold medals dramatically discredited Adolf Hitler's racist claims. He demonstrated the feats a person can achieve regardless of race or origin—a message that also resonated at home, since segregation was still the norm in the United States.

HATTIE McDANIEL (circa 1895–1952)

A gifted radio and film actress, Hattie McDaniel was the first African American to win an Academy Award, for her portrayal of Mammy in the classic movie *Gone with the Wind* (1939). It is estimated that McDaniel acted in more than 300 films throughout her career, though she received on-screen credit for far fewer. Most of the roles available to a black woman in Hollywood in the 1930s and 1940s were those of a maid or a cook, and McDaniel increasingly came under fire—especially toward the end of her career—for the limited scope of her roles. But there can be no doubt that she set the stage for future minority actors and artists in Hollywood.

ELLA FITZGERALD (1917–1996)

Ella Fitzgerald's bright, effortless vocals and singular talent made her one of the greatest jazz singers of all time. After winning a talent competition at Harlem's celebrated

Apollo Theater when she was just sixteen, she went on to perform in bands and later as a solo singer. Nicknamed the "First Lady of Song," Ella is especially noted for her development of the vocal technique "scatting." Her numerous hit songs expanded beyond the borders of jazz and blues to include inventive and hugely popular interpretations of classic favorites by composers like Ira and George Gershwin and Cole Porter. Fitzgerald won thirteen Grammy Awards and is one of the bestselling recording artists in history.

JACKIE ROBINSON (1919–1972)

Ending years of segregation in U.S. sports, Jackie Robinson was the first African American to play baseball in the major leagues. Robinson was a standout athlete in high school and college, lettering at UCLA not just in baseball but also in football, basketball, and track. After serving in the army during World War II, Robinson went to play baseball in the Negro Leagues. From there, he was recruited to join the Brooklyn Dodgers, where he spent his entire career, breaking racial barriers as quickly as he broke athletic records. Among other awards and achievements, Robinson was the first African American to be inducted into the Baseball Hall of Fame. After he retired from sports, Robinson continued to lobby for racial equality and integration, writing letters to every U.S. president from 1956 until his death in 1972.

ROSA PARKS (1913–2005)

Often called "the mother of the modern civil rights movement," Rosa Parks made history in 1955 when she was arrested for refusing to give up her seat on a public bus to a white man. This quiet act of defiance generated the Montgomery bus boycott, which brought Martin Luther King Jr. to prominence. More broadly, her actions set off a fury of emotion across the country, bringing issues of racial inequality and segregation firmly into the spotlight. Parks devoted her life to social service and the civil rights movement, never hesitating to speak out. She received numerous awards for her efforts, including the Presidential Medal of Freedom and Congress's highest honor, the Congressional Gold Medal.

RUBY BRIDGES (1954–)

Proving that even the smallest members of society can make a big difference, Ruby Bridges was only six years old when she helped integrate the New Orleans public school system. In 1960, she became the first African American child to attend an all-white school in the South. Her brave walk to school, surrounded by U.S. marshals, was immortalized by Norman Rockwell in the painting *The Problem We All Live With*.

The school's integration caused the community to erupt in protest, and Bridges had to endure daily threats; only one teacher in the school was willing to teach her. As an adult, Bridges created the Ruby Bridges Foundation to promote tolerance through education.

MARTIN LUTHER KING JR. (1929–1968)

Arguably the most prominent of all civil rights activists, Martin Luther King Jr. started as a Baptist minister but ultimately preached to a global audience. During the 1950s and 1960s he demanded equality for African Americans, organizing peaceful protests and inspiring a nation through his speeches. The most famous was his "I Have a Dream" speech, which he gave to more than 200,000 demonstrators at the March on Washington in 1963. In 1964, King became the youngest recipient of the Nobel Peace Prize; he was awarded the Congressional Gold Medal after his death. King was tragically assassinated in 1968, and his extraordinary contribution to our country is commemorated every January by a national holiday.

THURGOOD MARSHALL (1908–1993)

The first black justice of the U.S. Supreme Court, Thurgood Marshall courageously legislated for equality for African Americans and all minorities, influencing numerous landmark cases. He spent more than twenty years as the head lawyer for the National Association for the Advancement of Colored People (NAACP). It was in this role in 1954 that he successfully tried the historic *Brown v. Board of Education* case, defeating the "separate but equal" doctrine by ending segregation in public schools. President Lyndon B. Johnson appointed Marshall to the Supreme Court in 1967, where he continued to challenge discrimination in all forms.

BARACK OBAMA (1961–)

The first African American elected to the nation's highest office, Barack Obama became the forty-fourth president of the United States on January 20, 2009. Running a campaign that heralded change, Obama energized a young voting population and beat out Republican senator John McCain in the general election. Prior to becoming president, Obama served as a U.S. senator and an Illinois state senator. Obama is also an author, and in law school he became the first African American to serve as president of the *Harvard Law Review*.

About the Illustrators

COZBI A. CABRERA's beautiful, handcrafted cloth dolls have garnered the attention of collectors around the world. She attended Parsons School of Design and lives in Brooklyn, New York. Cozbi has illustrated *Beauty, Her Basket*; *Thanks a Million*; *Most Loved in All the World*; and *Stitchin' and Pullin': A Gee's Bend Quilt*.

"I have always been drawn to Rosa Parks's quiet strength."

R. GREGORY CHRISTIE is a Brooklyn-based, multiple award-winning children's book illustrator who visits schools all over the country. www.gas-art.com

"I was interested in contributing to this book because the simple, few words of this poem can fill volumes with their meaning."

BRYAN COLLIER is the Caldecott Honor and Coretta Scott King Award-winning illustrator of numerous children's books, including *Rosa* and *Martin's Big Words: The Life of Dr. Martin Luther King, Jr.* When he's not painting, he spends his time visiting schools and encouraging young artists and readers. Bryan lives in New York with his wife and daughter. www.bryancollier.com

"This book is a celebration of strong, courageous men and women who truly understood service and sacrifice. My head and heart soar upward because the links in our history chain are so strong."

PAT CUMMINGS was raised as an Army "brat" in Germany, Okinawa, and Kansas, using art as an entrée whenever she moved from school to school. Having created everything from board books to teen novels, from nonfiction to children's television, she now teaches a children's book course at Parsons School of Design and at her alma mater, Pratt Institute.

"Even before I learned about Ella Fitzgerald's history, I considered the singular, pure clarity of her voice *transformative*: it contains all of the richness of her story—a very American story—and it actually has the power to improve whoever listens."

LEO AND DIANE DILLON, a husband-and-wife team, have collaborated on more than fifty picture and chapter books. They are known for their wide range of media and techniques and their mission to include people of many cultures in their work. They are the only artists to have received the Caldecott Medal two years in succession.

"We are very impressed by and respectful of George Washington Carver's accomplishments in an environment that was so hostile at that time. He is amazing."

AG FORD grew up in Dallas, Texas. At a young age he discovered his artistic ability, which later led him to the Columbus College of Art and Design. Ford's first picture book, *Barack* by Jonah Winter, reached the *New York Times* bestseller list. www.agfordillustration.com

"Jesse Owens's hard work, dedication, and passion for running inspire me to apply the same ideas to creating art."

E. B. Lewis received a Caldecott Honor for *Coming On Home Soon* by Jacqueline Woodson and the Coretta Scott King Illustrator Award for *Talkin' About Bessie* by Nikki Grimes. He teaches illustration at Philadelphia's University of the Arts and lives in Folsom, New Jersey.

"It is an amazing time to be alive."

Frank Morrison received the Coretta Scott King John Steptoe Award for his first children's book, *Jazzy Miz Mozetta* by Brenda C. Roberts. His unique style of painting is drawn from his extraordinary life experiences. Frank resides in Atlanta, Georgia, with his wife, Connie, their daughter, Nia, and three sons, Nyree, Tyreek, and Nasir. www.morrisongraphics.com

"As I worked, John Coltrane sounded through my speakers. I couldn't help but think of my ancestors. They didn't have the opportunities, the honors, the awards. They didn't have the promise of change, or the hope. I paint. This is my way of keeping the dreams alive. I paint for Martin, Coretta, and all the other Kings and Queens before me. I paint."

James Ransome is the illustrator of more than forty books and the winner of numerous awards. His work is part of both public and private children's book art collections. He teaches at Syracuse University and lives in Rhinebeck, New York, with his wife, writer Lesa Cline Ransome, and their children.

"This line of text opened to me all the broad and complicated ways our ancestors fought: the wars that blacks have been involved in, violent slave rebellions, and more subtle day-to-day undertakings."

Charlotte Riley-Webb has won numerous awards as a fine artist, including a Pollock-Krasner Foundation award. Charlotte has also illustrated several children's books, including *Rent Party Jazz*, *Sweet Potato Pie*, *The Entrance Place of Wonders*, and the upcoming *I Like Brown*. She lives in Georgia. www.charlotterileywebb.com

"Much of the civil rights struggle was fought in the South, and Jackie Robinson was a positive source of strength, talent, and endurance, accomplishing many of his outstanding victories on Southern baseball fields."

Shadra Strickland, a native of Atlanta, Georgia, studied illustration and design at Syracuse University and earned her MFA at New York's School of Visual Arts. Her first book, *Bird*, received the Coretta Scott King John Steptoe Award and was named a *Kirkus Reviews* Best Children's Book. She currently resides in Brooklyn, New York.

"The extraordinary courage of Ruby Bridges and her family in leading school integration in the South made whites and blacks understand how similar we all are in our hopes for our children. It was pivotal in moving the country forward in understanding, tolerance, and, ultimately, love."

Eric Velasquez was born in Spanish Harlem, New York, and earned his BFA from the School of Visual Arts. He has illustrated more than fourteen picture books, including *Grandma's Records*, which he also authored. He lives in Hartsdale, New York.

"Barack Obama's campaign was a historic and inspirational moment for me."